I Am the Invisible Kind

Clea Saal

Table of Contents

1. A Word We Don't Say

Gay or straight? Maybe bi? Trans? These are all identities we keep hearing about on a daily basis. They are literally everywhere. We live in a world that seems to be obsessed with sex, gender, and gender identity, so we can't even take two steps without tripping over half a dozen references to them. Maybe we are just trying to make up for lost time, as it was only a few decades ago that these words were basically taboo, ones we barely dared whisper. My, how have things changed, and for the most part I would say it has been for the better, as we try to figure out how to build a more inclusive society; as gay rights, and trans rights at long last come to be seen as basic human rights. You know who is missing, who remains invisible and unmentioned? Those of us who describe ourselves as asexual.

It is a funny twist of fate, as up until not too long ago a sort of 'public asexuality' was both expected and demanded. Sure, people were dating, they were falling in and out of love, they were most definitely having sex, and they were making babies, that was a given (as it was also a given that the people who were dating, falling in and out of love, having sex, and making babies were straight, which goes to show just how much was going unacknowledged... okay, so for the most part the whole making babies thing *was* indeed limited to straight couples, as biology has always been kind of biased in that regard, and assisted reproductive technologies were a nascent field, one in which it was not uncommon for doctors to openly discriminate against single women and same sex couples). It just wasn't something we talked about, and even public displays of affection among straight couples were kind of frowned upon. Sex was supposed to be a private matter, it was supposed to be kept strictly behind closed doors, and safely out of sight... and in that context it was ridiculously easy for asexuality to slip by unnoticed.

In fact, having grown up in a world that predated the advent of the internet, one in which our access to information, and our ability to connect with others, were far more limited than they are today, I never even came across the word asexual until I was well into my thirties, not in this particular context. It just wasn't part of my vocabulary, nor was it part of that of those around me. I just knew I was weird. I knew I didn't fit, but there was no term I could reach out to explain why, no label I could apply to myself... and no, contrary to what some may be inclined to believe, I don't come from a conservative or religious family, where the subject was taboo, quite the contrary. It's just that we have a tendency to forget that only a couple of decades ago things were different... very, *very*, *VERY* different.

How different? Well, both of my parents were mental health professionals, with the accompanying obsession with the subject of sex, gender, and the like —they were both psychoanalysts, to be accurate, meaning that everything, and I do mean absolutely *everything* I, or anyone else, did was seen through the prism of sex— so the subject itself was normalized in my family to an extent it was not in the average household, not in those days. Now, whether that understanding was healthy, or even made sense, is open for debate (what can I say? As far as I am concerned, their views on the matter, especially my dad's, were a little too rooted on the nineteenth century's perception of gender roles for comfort... Freud and all that. I mean, I remember getting a long and rambling talk from my father on the subject of penis envy when I was something like thirteen years old. No, the guy never quite got the hang of the concept of 'age appropriate'. Of course, to be fair, if you were to ask me, I would probably say that the right time for that particular conversation was exactly never, but that's a different matter), but the point I was trying to make is that I grew up surrounded by references to the subject, and I also grew up surrounded, and being fully aware of, my parents' openly gay friends. It wasn't just that my parents *had* those friends in the first place (yes, now we may see that as a given, but as much as we may want to deny it, back in the seventies that was most definitely not the norm), but also the fact that I was never 'shielded' from the nature of those relationships, and to me there was nothing unusual about them at all.

The thing is that, unlike too many of my peers, I never feared I would be rejected if I were to come out as a lesbian, or as bi (though trans would have been pushing it), but asexual? I don't think the notion ever even crossed my parents' minds (especially my father's, who I'm not sure has figured it out to this day, and I am over fifty years old. My mom? I lost her when I was in my twenties, before the word asexual entered even my own vocabulary, but I suspect she had at least an inkling of what was going on in that regard, as she made more than one comment about my cynicism, and how I seemed to have given up on love and romance without even trying them, and had come out on the other side, but back to my story). The point I was trying to make is that even for a couple of sex obsessed psychoanalysts the concept just wasn't part of their mental landscape. It was not something I am sure they could even begin to wrap their minds around. As far as they were concerned sexual desire was the driving force behind all of human interaction, the be all and end all of human existence, the subtext that explained everything. It was their chosen filter.

Yes, the universe *does* have a sense of humor. They thought they were ready for everything, and then their one and only daughter turned out to fall into the one category they couldn't even begin to comprehend.

The thing is that being asexual can be described as a double edged sword.

On the one hand there is the fact that it is the one unconventional identity that can't possibly be legally discriminated against (though just as has been the case for the members of other minorities, we have always had to deal with the social pressure to conform to societal norms; to get married, make babies, and so on), on the other there is the fact that, in a really twisted kind of way, it is the most unusual of them all.

We humans are supposed to share a number of basic biological needs with the rest of the animal kingdom. The need to eat, the need to sleep (okay, so this one may be a little iffier, as it is hard to say that an oyster, a sea sponge, or a jellyfish, which have no brains at all, are awake, and some argue that sleep is restricted to species with eyelids, so there go the fish too), and, for the most part, the need to pass down our genes through sexual reproduction (a trait that is indeed shared by fish and oysters, though jellyfish and sea sponges are a little iffier in that regard, as most of their species reproduce asexually). The thing is that while we humans (and most mammals, birds, reptiles, amphibians and the like) would die without food, water, and in some instances sleep, we can get by without sex just fine if need be. It is just that for most humans the very notion is unthinkable. Yes, some may be attracted to the 'wrong' partners by society's, and even biology's, standards (and that can, and often does, cause some discomfort among those who still see them as something alien, and openly discriminate against them), but they are still attracted to *someone*, they are still guided by the same primal imperative. They may be bending the rules a bit, they may even be said to be cheating, but at least they are still playing something resembling the same basic game. We, on the other hand, are sitting on the sidelines, eating popcorn, and watching the whole thing unfold.

We are *The Dreaming Jewels*.

Okay, so I realize that not everyone is an sf nutcase, and that the reference is a fairly obscure one, so where does that particular term come from, and what does it mean? It comes from the title of a book by Theodore Sturgeon that was published in 1950. Without giving away too much of the plot, in it there are these alien (or rather alien-like) lifeforms that have shared the earth with us since time immemorial, but whose life is based on principles that are so utterly different from our own that their existence has effectively gone unnoticed.

Now, I freely admit I'm just me, and I can't speak for the asexual community as a whole, if it is even possible to speak of such a thing. I am asexual, but that does not define me. It is not something that guides my every thought, and my every action. It is just another adjective. It is a label that makes it easier for me to understand *why* I don't fit, what sets me apart. It is also one that makes it easier for me to get others to understand just where it is that I am coming from. I suspect that for others it may be the same, or maybe it is not. I just don't know, and even writing these words feels kind of awkward. As I said, it is not something I spend much time thinking about, but whether I like it or not —and whether I am aware of it or not— I suspect it is something that does have a significant impact on the ways in which I interact with others. Yes, there is a growing awareness of the fact that we are out there, that we actually exist, but in spite of that we are still invisible, we are still dismissed.

People may speak of a gay radar, or something along those lines, but there is no asexual radar, not that I know of, or if there is mine is most definitely broken (unfortunately after more than half a century of use I am also fairly certain that its warranty has long since expired).

The thing is that while we can't be easily discriminated against —not like gay, bi and trans people can be— we can all too easily be overlooked. We can, and often do, get lost in the shuffle, so here goes my attempt to carve a small space for myself, and maybe to help others to understand just where is it that I am (or maybe I should say we are) coming from, because one thing I have come to realize is that I'm not the only one, that I am not alone... it just feels that way.

2. And Then They F*cked

'And they lived happily ever after', so is supposed to end pretty much every fairy tale under the sun, or so we are told (okay, so quite a few of them are far bleaker than that, have a look at Hans Christian Andersen's *The Little Match Girl* if you don't believe me, but let's stick with the Disneyfied version for the time being). You know what that 'and they lived happily ever after' is? Of course you do, it is a very pretty euphemism, one that translates roughly as 'and then they f*cked'. That is what, when you get down to it, the term actually entails. It is the point of the game, what we are supposed to be here on this earth for, and we better not forget it. We are here to make babies, we are literally put on this planet to have sex... or at least that is the official party line, the one we have drilled into our skulls from the day we are born, whether we are aware of it, or not.

It is also what most books, movies and songs are about, which, when you think about it, is not particularly surprising.

In some cultures a person's life is not considered complete until he or she sees his or her first grandchild being born. That, rather than the birth of their first child, is the defining moment, the confirmation that the cycle will go on. It is the final sign that serves to demonstrate that they have actually made it, and in a way it makes sense (and it made even more sense back when child and infant mortality rates were in the mid double digits, which explains the emphasis on grandchildren rather than children). Richard Dawkins has described living beings as 'throwaway survival machines for genes', and what do those genes need us to do in order to survive? They need us to make babies, they need us to have sex. Everything else is irrelevant.

Now, it is true that we humans don't always play by the rules, and that people in the ace spectrum are not alone in sidestepping that one. That the same holds true, out of necessity, for plenty of gay (and to a slightly lesser extent lesbian) couples, to say nothing of the countless couples who are struggling with infertility, and for those who are simply childfree by choice (both those who buy into the whole DINK, i.e. Double Income, No Kids lifestyle, and those who are concerned about the state of our planet, and who feel that, considering how things are going, the best gift they can give their future children is not to have any). What sets us asexuals apart is that while gay couples, as well as those dealing with infertility, or even the ones making a deliberate choice not to have kids, either can't get, or don't want to reach, the intended goal, asexuals just shrug the very notion of playing the game aside... and it is around this game that society as a whole is organized.

It is at the center of everything, and the reminders are all but inescapable. The messaging is relentless, and it begins long before we are even aware of what it actually entails, meaning that we are also in no position to even *try* to fight it. We just take it in, one bit at a time.

I freely admit that when I go (or, let's be honest here, went) to the movies I used to wonder if maybe I shouldn't get a thirty percent discount, figuring that I was bound to spend something like a third of the film openly rolling my eyes, and wondering when were they going to get back to the story anyways. That is also one of the reasons I tend to gravitate towards old time science fiction, animation, and the classics. Those are my safe spaces, to the extent that there are any. Even a romantic comedy such as *Singin' in the Rain* or *Some Like It Hot*, has enough of a plot outside the love story to make it fun to watch. Yes, there is that inescapable 'and then they f*cked' subtext lurking in the background, but back in those days that subtext had the sense to stay in the background. Nowadays? Nowadays directors seem to be determined to cram it down our throats, replacing subtlety and storytelling with as many sex scenes as they can possibly get away within the time that they have been allotted, while the story is little more than an excuse, and subtlety has basically been thrown out the window.

Oh, I do realize that there was a time, back in the 60s and 70s, when this whole thing made a certain amount of sense, as directors were trying to get rid of the shackles of what had been the prudish laws that had characterized the film industry up to that point, and were desperate to see how far the boundaries could be pushed, but nowadays? Nowadays there is nothing edgy about the whole thing, not any more. The boundaries have been pushed as far as they will go, in fact they have been obliterated into nothing, so this is no longer about pushing boundaries. Now it is all about pushing our buttons.

It is about the fact that sex sells, and at the end of the day they figure that the more sex scenes they cram into their films, the more butts they will cram into those theater seats.

Yes, I know we asexuals are the exception, and we can't expect the rest of the world to cater to our sensitivities. I get that ninety-nine percent of the population finds the subject of sex to be absolutely fascinating in one way or another (that's precisely why sex sells), and when I say they find it fascinating I don't just mean like an entomologist observing the unusual coloration of a particular beetle, which is how I feel about the whole thing more often than not.

As for books and music, well, I can appreciate a love song as much as anyone, even if I can't fully relate, and I'll even go so far as to admit that a fairly provocative tune with a title such as *Fat Bottomed Girls* can be catchy enough to hold my interest... and yes, I can have fun listening to something like that without openly rolling my eyes, but at the end of the day I am still here mostly for the music, and not lusting after the artists, so I do find most fans reactions to be kind of silly. Of course, the fact that, unlike movies, songs are usually only a few minutes long also means that they don't drag on forever, and more often than not they don't have much of a plot either, but serve instead as rather ridiculous proclamations of love. For the most part they all boil down to something along the lines of 'I love you, I love you, I really really love you', the edgier 'I love you, I love you, I really really love you, and we are going to have so much fun doing X, Y and Z together', or the bleaker side 'I loved you, I loved you so much, but you dumped me, and I just can't get over you' and then we are done. We are free to move on, though we also have things like Ugly Kid Joe's *Everything About You,* an utterly obscure tune that came out back in the early nineties, before the positivity police was in full swing. Now I'm not sure anyone would be able to get away with releasing such a 'love song' because someone somewhere is bound to take offense, and call it triggering.

And then there are the books...

Okay, so maybe books should come first, as they do predate movies by several centuries, and it is true that there are plenty of classics where this is not such a relevant factor (or books where it not only is a relevant factor, but that also have a tendency to shatter our expectations with regards to a given era we tend to perceive as repressed and demure, think of how well Bocaccio's *Decameron,* or Chaucer's *Canterbury Tales* fit with our preconceived notions of the Middle Ages if you don't believe me), but for the most part, once again we are basically stuck. Heck, even Homer's *Odyssey* ends with a good old-fashioned 'and then they f*cked', they just take a bit longer to get to that point. Of course, the fact that books have been around since the dawn of history, or thereabouts —after all the beginning of history itself is defined by the appearance of writing, anything that predates it is lumped into prehistory — means that we have a wider range of choices, and we are more likely to find something that suits our needs.

As I've mentioned before, I tend to gravitate towards things like classic sf, fantasy, and also books that have traditionally been read by children (though not necessarily books that were written with children in mind, as the notion of writing a book specifically for that crowd is a fairly modern one, so we have things like *Robinson Crusoe*, or *Gulliver's Travels*, that have long since been lumped into this category, but that is more by chance than by design). As for classic fantasy and sf... well, that was officially aimed a chaste young men (yeah, right), so the sexual content is never explicit, though sometimes they go to the opposite end of the spectrum, and wind up excluding female characters altogether. That is nowhere as clearly exemplified as in J.R.R. Tolkien's *Lord of the Rings* trilogy, or *The Hobbit*. And yes, just like asexual characters are few and far between throughout history, so seem to be women in the science fiction of the fifties and sixties (think Isaac Asimov, Ray Bradbury, and the like), though that does not necessarily apply to the science fiction of an earlier era, especially British science fiction, where we find things such as Olaf Stapleton's *Sirius* (that one dates back to 1944, and let's just say that while in the end the boy does get the girl... well, the takeaway message makes it clear that said boy wouldn't necessarily have been her first choice. Er, yes, that is one book that, upon a closer and less prudish reading, does have some less than subtle undertones, though maybe calling them 'undertones' is a bit of a stretch, as they are pretty close to the surface, and about as subtle as an anvil falling on your head), or the hedonistic and dystopian view of the future we encounter in Aldous Huxley's *Brave New World*, which actually dates back to the early thirties, and depicts a world in which sexual gratification is both expected, and readily available (in fact refusal to participate is utterly unacceptable, to the point that children are deliberately conditioned to join in from their earliest childhood, and actively punished if they refuse to do so), but deeper personal connections have all but vanished. Thank God that never came to pass!

3. An Atheist at a Religious Gathering

Sometimes I feel as if being asexual in this day and age were akin to being an atheist at a gathering of religious fundamentalists.

Yes, there are a number of contingents out there, and just like Christians, Jews, and Muslims those contingents don't always get along, but at the end of the day they share a common foundation. They may worship in different ways, and disagree on pretty much everything (and the smaller the difference, the bigger the fuss they are likely to make about it, or so it seems), but at the end of the day there is one point they can all agree on: the fact that there is some sort of God out there. Asexuals are like a bunch of atheists suddenly showing up and saying 'Um?'

It may not be the most articulate of introductions, but just by showing up those atheists are throwing a huge wrench into the inner workings of things. They are questioning the one point on which everyone seemed to agree, the one they all take for granted, and that is not a position that is likely to be appreciated, and much less welcomed.

Another aspect in which asexuals can be seen as a counterpart of atheists is in the fact that they don't have the sense of community that seems to characterize religious groups, nor does there seem to be a concerted effort to create safe or shared spaces. Christians go to church, Jews have their synagogues, just as Muslims have their mosques. Buddhists too have their temples. Atheists? Nope, there is no formally acknowledged place for them to gather, that would make no sense... and the same holds true for what passes for the asexual community. Heterosexuals have always been acknowledged and respected. They effectively rule the roost. They are like the Christians of Medieval Europe. Gays, lesbians, and the like have fought like hell to open some spaces up for themselves. They have earned them the hard way, just as women did (in a not entirely different context) a few decades prior. Asexuals? They haven't even gotten started, and they are unlikely to feel the same pressing need.

That, I suspect, goes back to something I mentioned in the opening chapter of this book (though I am extremely reluctant to speak for the asexual community, such as it is), and that is the fact that we don't see our asexuality as our main defining characteristic. I can't escape the fact that I am a woman, and that fact has shaped my everyday experience of the world around me in a very visible way. My asexuality? That one too has most definitely left its mark, but while one defines how the world sees me, the other does not.

Unlike all other forms of sexual expression and identity, asexuality is an utterly invisible trait, one that is all but devoid of external manifestations. We are not defined by what we do, but rather by what we *don't* do.

In theology there is a concept known as the *via negativa*. It means to define something in terms of what it is not, rather than of what it is. It is a concept that can be found across time and space, and it is usually reserved for those things we can never fully hope to comprehend (and while it is a concept that has traditionally been associated with theology, where God is often described as unknowable, it is not entirely confined to religious studies). The *via negativa* is not restricted to a single tradition either, so let's take a look at a couple of examples of what it actually entails.

The most obvious of these is to be found in the opening lines of the *Tao Te Ching*, the foundational text of Taoism, which begins as follows:

> *The Tao [the way] that can be described is not the*
> *enduring and unchanging Tao [way].*
> *The name that can be named is not the enduring*
> *and unchanging name.*

On the Christian side of things, where the via negativa is a bit less common, we have that during the course of the ninth century the theologian Johannes Scotus Eriugena wrote the following:

> *We do not know what God is. God Himself does*
> *not know what He is because He is not anything*
> *[i.e., 'He is not any created thing']. Literally God*
> *is not, because He transcends being.*

The best known manifestation of the *via negativa*, on the other hand, can probably be traced back to India, to texts such as the *Upanishads*, and the *Avadhuta Gita* (*The Song of the Free Soul*) where we encounter the concept of neti neti ('not this, not this', or 'not this, not that' depending on the translation), which often seeks to define Brahman and/or the soul based on what they are not, rather than on what they are, and then of course there is

Buddhism, which has the concept of anatta, the denial of the very existence of the self, or of a truly unchangeable essence of a person, as its foundational principle. You can think of it as 'you are not your body, you are not your mind', a concept that opposes the more traditional, or perhaps intuitive, view that says 'I am my body, I am my mind' even though at the end of the day you sort of know that that's not entirely true, that you are actually neither, or maybe that you are more than the sum of those parts. Of course, the question that remains is what are you, but that, that cannot really be defined, which is sort of the whole point of this exercise because at the end of the day the very ability of words to describe things is too limited to be able to truly define what is unlimited.

An interesting example from the *Avadhuta Gita* is the following (and before we go any further I sort of want to apologize for the length of this one, as neti neti was refusing to stay put, coming and going as it saw fit, and in the end I decided to include the whole thing, figuring that it was better than a whole bunch of unconnected bits and pieces that don't really mean much, but yeah, the whole thing gets kind of rambling, at least for the purposes of this book, so sorry about that!):

All the scriptures say that the Truth is without attributes, pure, immutable, bodiless, and existing equally everywhere. Know me to be That.

Know that which has form to be false, that which is formless to be eternal. Through the instruction of this truth there is no longer rebirth into this world.

Sages say that Reality is one only and the same. And through renunciation of attachment, the mind, which is one and many, ceases to exist.

If it is of the nature of the not-Self, how can there be Samadhi? If it is of the nature of the Self, how can there be Samadhi? If it is both "is" and "is not", how can there be Samadhi [union with the divine]?

You are pure homogeneous Reality, disembodied, unborn, and immutable. Why do you think of yourself as "I know it here" or as "I do not know"?

By such sentences as "That thou art," our own Self is affirmed. Of that which is untrue and composed of the five elements - the Sruti (scripture) says, "Not this, not this."

As the self is filled by the Self, so is all filled continuously by you. There is no meditator or meditation. Why does your mind meditate shamelessly?

I do not know the Supreme; how shall I speak of Him?I do not know the Supreme how shall I worship Him? If I am the supreme One, who is the highest Truth, who is homogeneous Being and like unto space, how then shall I speak of Him and worship Him?

The principle of ego is not the Truth, which is homogeneous, which is free from the cause of superimposition and distinctions of perceived and perceiver. How can the ego be That which is aware of Itself?

There is no substance whatever which is by nature unlimited. There is no substance whatever which is of the nature of Reality. The very Self is the supreme Truth. There is neither injury nor non injury in It.

You are the homogeneous Reality; you are pure, bodiless, birthless, and imperishable. Why then do you have any delusion about the Self? Again, why am I myself deluded?

When the pot is broken, the space within it is absorbed in the infinite space and becomes undifferentiated. When the mind becomes pure, I do not perceive any difference between the mind and the supreme Being.

There is no pot; there is no pot's interior space. Neither is there an individual soul nor the form of an individual soul. Know the absolute Brahman, devoid of knowable and knower

And now back to our story. I guess the point I was trying to make is that I am not gay, not straight, not trans, and to be perfectly honest, not interested.

4. From Normal to Abnormal

If you look at it from the outside, the way in which the tables have turned is kind of funny. If you are stuck in the middle of it, not so much.

In a nutshell, back in the bad old days, when sex was a taboo subject, we asexuals had it easy. No, we were not rubbing our existence on anyone else's faces, we were not more vocal about our sexuality, or lack thereof, than the rest of the world (in fact some, and maybe even most, of us didn't even know *what* we were). It is just that as long as the subject was one that was not to be mentioned in polite company, we were fine. That unlike what happened to be the case for pretty much everyone else, that was just down our alley. As I have mentioned before, we are, and have always been, the one sexual minority that couldn't, and still can't, be officially criminalized and persecuted for the simple reason that in order to do that you would have to make *not* having sex into a criminal offense, and that is not exactly feasible. Yes, we were lucky.

In fact, when it came to the condemnation of non-traditional sexual identities, even 'medical science' got in on the act, and up until ridiculously recently both homosexuality and transsexuality (or to be accurate gender dysphoria) were officially classified as mental illnesses, which goes to show just how reliable that particular label happens to be, and to what extent it can be twisted to respond to the whims of society, rather than to an actual medical need. Now, that is not to say that mental illnesses are not real, that things such as schizophrenia and psychotic behavior are not serious conditions that require medical intervention, but there are also a whole bunch of other diagnoses that are floating around that either translate into 'doesn't fit and/or refuses to comply', or describe behaviors that, while potentially lethal —such as self-harm and suicidal ideations— refer to states of mind where the label of 'illness' is likely to do more harm than good.

But now let's get back to the two labels that concern us: homosexuality and gender dysphoria.

Up until how recently were those two deemed to be forms of mental illness? Well, when it comes to homosexuality it wasn't until 1973 that the American Psychiatric Association removed it from the official list of diagnoses, while the World Health Organization didn't follow suit until 1990.

That is the medical perspective, now let's have a look at the legal one. How fast, and how far, have things changed in that regard?

Well, there we have that in 1952 Alan Turing was convicted of 'gross indecency' in the United Kingdom. He was given a choice between incarceration and probation, though said probation, which is what he ultimately chose, required him to undergo what was effectively a form of chemical castration. Two years later he was dead by his own hand, as the changes he could see in his body were more than he could stand. He would eventually go on to receive a posthumous 'pardon' (we could argue whether he needed pardoning at all, or if it was society as a whole that should have been proffering an apology on bended knee, one that, being dead, the guy was in no position to accept, but let's not focus on the details). Today his face adorns the new £50.00 bill.

When it comes to the United States, there we have that in the 1950s all fifty states had some sort of anti-sodomy law, and in 1986, even as these laws were being stricken off the books left, right and center, the supreme court upheld the right of states to declare homosexuality illegal. In fact it wasn't until 2003, thirty years after the APA stopped classifying it as a form of mental illness, that the decision was made that these laws contravened the most basic of individual freedoms, and they were finally declared unconstitutional, though they remain officially in the books in some fourteen states to this day. That decriminalization? It came less than one year before Massachusetts would go on to become the first state to actually legalize same sex marriage (and a couple of years *after* the Netherlands became the first country to officially perform and recognize such unions). That is how different the attitudes in the different regions happened to be, and at a global level still are. As of this writing, there are something like seventy countries (out of 195) where homosexuality remains illegal, including a number of majority Muslim countries in which it is actually a capital offense. Granted, many of those seventy countries are former British colonies, such as Jamaica, where these laws are rarely, if ever, enforced, but they remain in the books, and that is a troubling thought.

As for gender dysphoria? That one wasn't taken off the list of disorders in the United States until 2013, and the World Health Organization kept it in the books as an official diagnosis until 2019. Of course, that one also opens up an entirely different can of worms, because while listing it as a mental disorder as the term has been traditionally understood is no longer acceptable (and let's be clear that what we are talking about here is a response by mainstream society towards a behavior that seems to deviate from what is deemed to be 'the norm', rather than any sort of disease), it did, and still does, have a number of characteristics that make it particularly tricky. The reason? Well, because while in order for homosexuality to become at least nominally accepted 'all' that was needed was an attitude adjustment (or at least that is the theory), when it comes to gender dysphoria what we are talking about is a condition that went from being seen as something to be suppressed, to one that requires an active supportive medical intervention in the form of hormone therapy, and gender confirmation surgery, to say nothing of other legal accommodations. It is not, in other words, a situation where all we have to do to make things right is pat someone on the head, and say 'hey, you're good to go now, sorry about that!'

In addition to that there is also the fact that from the day we are born, on our birth certificates, we are assigned a specific gender based on our anatomical characteristics: either male or female. For the vast majority of us that is a non-issue, and that holds true even for gays and lesbians, but for those suffering from gender dysphoria that label is a heavy burden that, depending on where they live, or where they happened to be born, they may have no choice but to shoulder for as long as they live. It is a misidentification that cuts deep. In some countries there are few, if any, legal hurdles when it comes to straightening out this particular mess, others require judicial intervention, a medical diagnosis, or even gender confirmation surgery. In quite a few it is illegal no matter what. As for the United States, what we have here is, as is too often the case, a patchwork of legislations that can be all but impossible to navigate or reconcile.

Of course, the problem is not just about the law, as there are some countries/territories, such as Chechnya, where the extrajudicial killing of gay and transexual men is a common practice, as is the 'corrective rape' of lesbians, while the authorities turn a deliberately blind eye. It is a scenario that plays itself out across the globe day in and day out, something that is worth keeping in mind, especially because more often than not we find ourselves in a bubble that tends to treat the attitudes we see reflected in progressive circles in the West as the norm. Out in the real world this is most definitely *not* the case.

It is a problem, one that must be addressed, and an area where there remains quite a bit of work that needs to be done, but now let's get back to the subject of this particular book, because while the world (or at least some parts of it) finally seems to be moving in the right direction in that regard, with several countries having not only legalized same sex marriage, and enacted a number of protections, but also going so far as to make it illegal to treat gender identity issues as a mental disorder, to say nothing of the banning of practices such as conversion therapy, at times it feels like asexuality is moving in the opposite direction.

No, there is no way it can ever be declared illegal, or anything like that (and it is also unlikely to ever come to be seen as pathological in the way homosexuality and gender dysphoria were until not too long ago), but this is not just about the law, it is about so much more than that. For instance it is not uncommon to find that the status of gays, lesbians and transexuals in a given country does not match what the law says, and for the attitudes out on the streets to remain openly hostile. In Ecuador, for instance, same sex marriage has been legal for a number of years now, discrimination and pathologization are officially outlawed, and transgender individuals can change their registration in their official identity documents without the need for surgery, or any sort of judicial authorization, but something between one half and two thirds of the population remains opposed even to the notion of same sex marriage, which is seen as an alien policy that has been imposed from above (one that came about as a consequence of a decision by the supreme court), and is at odds with the country's own values. The thing is that, as the different forms of gender expression become normalized, out in the real world the absence of one is coming to be seen as more and more of an outlier.

Sex has gone from being a taboo subject we barely dared mention, to being the prism through which we see absolutely everything, and under those circumstances it is not surprising that the absence from that prism is suddenly leaving this particular group looking disturbingly out of focus. We don't fit. We are missing something society, and even biology, deems absolutely essential... and yes, the almost instinctive reaction of most people when they come across the notion of asexuality for the very first time is to ask what the heck is wrong with us.

In a way it is more than a little ironic, because even as homosexuality, bisexuality, and transsexuality are normalized, and are finally acknowledged as part of the natural spectrum of human sexuality —and as countries pass laws banning the pathologization of these behaviors—asexuality, which up until fairly recently had basically been flying under the radar, is increasingly coming to be seen as 'a problem', with some mental health professionals going so far as to treat it as either a form of sexual dysfunction, or downright denying its existence, and deeming us to be the deluded victims of our own denial. They are utterly convinced that asexuality is the product of trauma, or shame, or whatever. They believe we are repressing our natural selves, or some such nonsense. Try that argument with homosexuality in this day and age, and see where that gets you. In fact, as I mentioned in the opening chapter, I never even mentioned my own asexuality to my father, and I'm not sure the guy ever even considered the possibility, but I suspect that if he ever reads these words, he is going to blame it on me having some sort of daddy issues, or something along those lines, and he will insist on refusing to acknowledge the fact that this is simply who I am. It is one of the reasons I've kept quiet for decades. Coming out as anything else would have been acceptable in his world, or at least I would have been able to count on him biting his tongue for fear of being seen as a bigot by his peers, but coming out as asexual? In today's environment that may turn out to be a much tougher challenge.

Yes, asexuality is weird, it is unusual, and it tends to make people uncomfortable. We get it that you don't get us. Some see us as unfeeling, while others wish we would just go away. They say asexuality is not a sexual orientation at all... um, okay, if it is not a sexual orientation, then what is it? Well, it is a choice, of course... so say quite a few of those activists who have spent decades working to get others to accept that homosexuality, bisexuality, and transsexuality are *not* a matter of choice, that that's just the way they are.

Now, don't get me wrong, I am not claiming that any of those are choices. I am fully aware that they are not, but I do find the double standard in the minds of some activists, to say nothing of a fair share of the members of the LGBTQ+ community, to be more than a little hypocritical. They are claiming for themselves the right to deny the validity of someone else's identity, of their sense of self, while demanding that their own be accepted without question, and that is something that does not sit well with me, but more on that in our next chapter.

5. 'A' Is for Ally

LGBT, make that LGBTQ... no, no, it's supposed to be LGBTQ+. That's still too vague, how about LGBTIQ, or LGBTQIA? Maybe LGBTTQQIAAP? That one doesn't exclude anyone! No, that's way too complicated, let's go back to LGBTQ, or maybe LGBTQIA+. Okay, but is the remaining T in that one for *transexual*, or does it stand for *transvestite*? Does the Q stand for *queer* or for *questioning*? And finally that A, is it for *ally* or for *asexual*? No, no, allies *must* come first. They are the ones who will stand by our side, shoulder to shoulder, while asexuals... well, those guys are just plain weird!

That, in a nutshell, is the infamous alphabet soup.

Okay, so maybe that was kind of tongue in cheek, or maybe just me being cheeky, but the truth is that I have long since given up on all hope of keeping on top of that one, as the acceptable form seems to change on a weekly (if not daily) basis, and woe be to those who fail to keep up... and of course there *is* a question as to just where do asexuals fit in this particular salad, with quite a few expressing doubts as to whether they belong at all, and in a way I do understand because at the end of the day we *are* an ill fit.

The whole point of this particular umbrella is supposed to be to provide cover for the different forms of sexual and gender identity and expression. It is all about pride, and moving forward. It is about people showing the world who they are, and demanding a space for themselves, and then along comes this one contingent, claiming a spot for itself in that coalition, but also saying 'fair enough, but can we *please* talk about something else, anything, because honestly, this obsession with sex? It's getting old', which is where the tension comes from, or at least part of it. In addition to that there is one thing I have mentioned a number of times already: the fact that we are much harder to openly discriminate against, and that at least until fairly recently we seemed to be doing just fine, thank you oh so very much. In fact it is only because the

LGBTQ+ community has struggled to make the subject one that is actually front and center that all of a sudden we find ourselves on the outskirts.

Oh, there have always been some challenges, and the isolation has always been a bit of an issue, as has been the fact that the very invisibility of asexuality, and the way in which the rest of the world seems to have a hard time wrapping their collective heads around the fact that we actually exist, has made interacting with others a lot harder than it should have been, but let's be honest here, anyone coming out as asexual would give rise to the dullest coming out party the world has ever seen. No one cares, and for the most part neither do we, and that in turn has given rise to the phenomenon known as asexual erasure, which is basically what we have here, and that *has* caused some resentment... some legitimate resentment.

The thing is that while the LGBTQ (or whatever the appropriate version of that acronym happens to be this week) community demands that we participate, that we be good *allies* if nothing else, that support is hardly ever reciprocated. We are treated as allies at best. That A is not ours, and we are still seen as outsiders who are expected to support them in their struggle, not as an interested party with its own concerns and priorities. We are not seen as a party that has a dog in this fight (as much as I am repulsed by the notion of dog fighting). In fact even within the context of the LGBTQ+ community some question whether asexuality should be classified as a sexual orientation at all. Add to that the fact that there are people on the ace spectrum who are not just not interested, but are actually sex repulsed, put those all together, and what you have is a recipe for disaster.

Let's be honest here, after centuries of being forced to stay in the closet, gays, lesbians, and transexuals have no intention of going back. In fact they want to be as open as possible, and quite a few of them delight in their newfound freedom to basically flaunt their sexuality. The problem is that while the members of those communities have an almost instinctive tendency to lash out against anyone reacting negatively to their very explicit manifestations of their sexuality, and their gender identity, the 'ew, gross!' that can often be heard coming from the asexual contingent is just as likely to be sexphobic. It is neither homophobic nor transphobic, that is not the issue, not from our perspective, but that is how members of the gay and trans community are likely to perceive it.

Yes, it may seem more than a little silly, in fact it can be almost embarrassing, but there are quite a few members of the ace community who retain that almost childlike response to the notion of sex... any sex. It is not something personal, but those who have long been discriminated against on that basis will almost inevitably see it that way, and they most definitely feel entitled to take offense at this perceived slight.

It is a situation where one side claims the right to be triggered by the reaction of the other, while denying the other side the right to be triggered by their own actions... and yes, I do see that as a double standard, as one side saying 'my triggers are valid and legitimate, and I expect you to respect them, but yours are not, so I will trample all over them'.

That can make coexistence under that supposedly shared umbrella more than a little awkward, but even saying that much is enough to make us sound like outsiders. We are not supposed to complain about it. We are just supposed to lend a shoulder, to grin and bear it, because at the end of the day 'we have it easy'.

In fact there are quite a few prominent members of the LGBTQ+ community who openly advocate for our exclusion on the grounds that we enjoy 'straight privilege', or who insist that our issues are unworthy of attention, and within the community itself those claims don't usually engender much (or any) backlash because there is a tendency for the members of that community to stick together, to defend each other through thick and thin.

That does leave us in an awkward position to say the least, dreading the notion of being seen as 'unsupportive of the cause' when it comes to gay rights, which is something most of us believe in, but also feeling rejected and dismissed, and wondering why should we even bother. Because it is the right thing? Yes, it is, and we will not get in your way, but when you then demand that we drop everything to support you, that we put you first, we are entitled to ask when will you support us in turn, when will you back *us* up.

I suspect most of us have had at least one of those friends who expects us to drop everything in order to be there for them in their time of need, but who are nowhere to be found when the situation is reversed... and we all know how those friendships tend to fare in the long run. The thing is that while we may end up coming to resent most of those so-called friends who are never actually there for us when we need them, it is not uncommon for those friends to be totally oblivious to what they are actually doing. They are just the kind of people who like to talk about themselves, and tune out the conversation when it turns to other subjects. They are like the friend who will spend twenty-seven minutes on the phone with you, going on and on about her current custody battle with her ex while knowing that your father is in the hospital, and where there is a very real possibility that he might have to be moved to the ICU, or worse, at any given moment, and never once considers the possibility of asking how he's doing (and yes, that is an actual example). Is her custody battle important? Yes, of course it is, and I most definitely understand that, as far as she is concerned, it is first and foremost in her mind, and I may want to do my best to support her, but you know what? For me the fact that my father is in the hospital may be just as pressing, and even if her ongoing custody battle is the most important issue in her mind, maybe her inquiring about my dad's health as a matter of common courtesy wouldn't be amiss. Would I ever testify against her? Of course not, nor would I ever wish for her to lose custody of her child, but if she keeps that up there will come a time where my reaction will be just an honest and heartfelt 'good luck'. I will no longer be willing to spend hours offering her a shoulder to cry on, or acting as a sounding board, or doing internet research on her behalf, or trying to offer any sort of advice, and I believe I would be justified in pulling back, not because not doing everything within my power to support her is the right thing to do, but rather because supporting her has become an exercise in frustration.

That is what I fear will end up happening between the asexual community (such as it is), and the very vocal LGBTQ+ contingent (especially its most vocal members)... and when it does we will almost certainly end up being demonized, and labeled as either homophobic or transphobic.

Yes, we are on the same side, or at least I think we are (for the most part), and I do believe that doing the right thing is important, but so is reciprocity, and its absence is causing more than a bit of tension here. You can't tell me that our fight is not one and the same, that my fight does not matter, and then demand that I set everything aside in order to take up arms on your behalf, and label my refusal to do so as some sort of a betrayal. That is not how allegiances work, not out in the real world.

No, at the end of the day, while we can try to carve a space for ourselves within the context of the LGBTQ+ community, we can't demand that we be accepted. It is their party, and they are allowed to turn us away if they want to, but we are also well within our rights to say that to us our issues come first, and that you can't dismiss us, and then turn around and complain that we are not sufficiently committed to what you have made clear is your, but not our, struggle.

Okay, so maybe it's not that simple. Yes, there are plenty of reasons for ace individuals to turn their backs on the LGBTQ+ community as a whole. For the most part they *have* proven themselves to be rather unreliable allies, and even in light of the fact that supporting them is 'the right thing to do', that attitude rankles. It does breed resentment. Those things are not mutually exclusive (and the fact that we are at a point where cancel culture means that any criticism of the LGBTQ+ community will be dismissed as either 'homophobic' or 'transphobic' without a second thought doesn't exactly help matters, as that automatic dismissal is not conductive to self-reflection). The problem is that these are categories that are far more fluid than their different labels (to say nothing of their most vocal activists) would seem to suggest, and well... let's just say that around the edges things can and do get muddled —that there are no armed guards patrolling the border, and checking your passport for a visa to cross from the land of the sexual to that of the asexual— and that in turn means that, while asexuals in the strictest sense of the word have not traditionally faced the same challenges that the LGBTQ+ community has always had to deal with, that to a large extent we have been shielded by our own invisibility, at the end of the day we cannot really draw such a line because, as we will see in the next chapter, the ace community is anything but monolithic. We are not defined by a single label, nor are we some sort of island that exists in total isolation. In fact we run a whole gamut, and that in turn means that their issues *are* indeed our issues... even if they keep trying to push us out of the way.

6. Shades of Grey

Black, grey, white, and some sort of purple. Those are the colors that, in a coalition represented by a rainbow flag, are meant to symbolize asexuality. It is not, as you can probably guess, the brightest and most cheerful of combinations. The black is supposed to be for asexuality itself. It is the void, the absence of color. Grey is, not surprisingly, for those who describe themselves as grey, meaning that they stand somewhere in the spectrum between sexuality and asexuality, bridging the gap. The white is supposed to represent either the allies or sexuality itself depending on who you ask (it doesn't help that the color white seems to be in quite a few of these flags, but also to take on a different meaning in each one of them), and purple is said to represent the asexual community as such.

Whatever. The point is that the one thing that flag makes absolutely clear, with its sequence of black, grey and white, is that there are different shades of grey bridging the gap between that black that represents the void that is deemed to be asexuality as such, and white, the shining light of full blown sexuality (and honestly, why that meaning of white would even be included in a flag that is supposed to represent the notion of asexuality is kind of baffling, but anyways). I admit I am not the biggest of fans, but then again I tend to find flags kind of silly as a matter of principle, and I wouldn't even have brought it up if it weren't for one thing: the prominence of the color grey, which, incidentally, is also to be found in the aromantic flag, which looks like an asexual flag upside down, only it has two shades of green replacing the color purple).

There are, by some counts, almost thirty flags out there (and that is not counting the variants of each one that may be floating around, as these things also have a tendency to evolve over time).

Anyway, as atomized as our understanding of sexual identity has become, it is not surprising that even asexuals can be further subdivided into a number of categories.

What we have in common is that we are not particularly interested in the prospect of having sex, and feel little, if any, sexual attraction or desire. On the other hand we are still human, and strange as it may seem to those who already see us as strange, the fact that we don't particularly care about the notion of having sex doesn't mean we want to spend our lives utterly alone (unfortunately that seems to be how things play out for too many of us, but that's another story). So now let's have a quick look at what's on the menu.

First of all we have those who are not just asexual, but also aromantic, meaning that they experience little to no romantic attraction towards anyone (and keep in mind that while the words asexual and aromantic are often seen walking hand in hand, there are people who feel sexual attraction, but not romantic attraction, so they do represent two clearly distinct categories that can in some instances be at odds with each other), but beyond that there are some who consider themselves heteroromantic, homoromantic, biromantic, and panromantic, all of which have their sexual counterparts, which can be readily identified (heterosexual for heteroromantic, homosexual for homoromantic, bisexual for biromantic, and so on). In addition to that we also have a whole bunch of shades of grey, reflecting the extent to which an individual experiences, or does not experience sexual attraction, and to top it all off we have the sex repulsed contingent (meaning those that not only don't experience sexual attraction, but are actually disgusted at the mere thought... oh, and to muddle things even further, the fact that someone is not just asexual, but also sex repulsed, doesn't necessarily mean that they are aromantic).

The number of possible combinations boggles the mind, but we are just getting started.

These shades of grey also refer to the extent to which any given individual is, or is not, willing to engage in sexual activity, and to further complicate matters keep in mind that there are also some individuals who have little to no interest in having sex themselves, and because of that they identify as asexual, but who are neither aromantic nor sex repulsed, and will do it to please their partners, because said partners are *not* asexual themselves (that whole not wanting to be alone thing again)... and in a way this is where we come full circle.

Remember how in the previous chapter at one point I mentioned that while for the most part the LGBTQ+ community has let us know in no uncertain terms that as far as they are concerned our struggle is not their struggle, and that they don't particularly care? Well, given that many of these members of the ace community who are asexual are neither aromantic nor sex repulsed, and that they may even be willing to engage in sexual activity for the sake of their non-ace partners while describing themselves as either homoromantic or biromantic, we end up coming to a point where our struggles once again overlap. Yes, the whole situation is kind of a mess.

Personally I think there comes a point where all these labels start getting in the way, that we are basically splitting hairs (in fact I suspect that that hairsplitting has had a lot to do with the tension between the ace contingent and the LGBTQ+ community as a whole). Now, whether or not a given individual is or is not aromantic and/or sex repulsed can be useful, but when we start referring to shades of grey in this particular spectrum... it can get to be a little too much. The whole point of identifying ourselves as part of a community is to find things we have in common, and, let's face it, when it comes to that one all this 'but I...' attitude is not particularly conductive.

Yes, we are all individuals, we all experience the world differently, and from our own perspectives, and we would like that individuality to be acknowledged, thank you oh so very much, but at the end of the day communities are all about generalizations. It is about what brings us together, not about what sets us apart. When you tell me how many spots are to be found on a given Dalmatian you are no longer describing dogs as a whole to me, you are describing a very specific dog... and this is about dogs in general, not about any freaking Dalmatian.

The thing is that, the purple in our flag notwithstanding, one of the things we asexuals seem to be missing is a sense of community (that whole being like an atheist in a gathering of religious fundamentalists thing again), but if we want that to change we have to understand that a community has to be about us, and what we have in common, not about me, and what makes me unique. That is something we have to leave at the door. We have enough problems, and enough trouble trying to get others to recognize the mere fact that we exist (or, worse yet, using our own differences to deny our existence), without us going out of our way to make it easier for them.

So yes, there is a spectrum there, and there are countless ways to define it, some more useful than others, but if we keep focusing on those we may well end up with one of those situations where we can no longer see the forest for the trees.

7. The 'Other' A-word

'What we've got here is, failure to communicate. Some men, you just can't reach'... okay, so maybe that is part of it, but what I am actually getting at is how mental health professionals, legal precedent, and evolving standards have managed to create something that can only be described as 'a mess'.

Now, before we go any further, I want to make it absolutely clear that when I refer to 'the *other* a-word' I don't mean a**hole, which is probably the first word that comes to mind when reading that particular title (and, yes, it is also one that often comes up), nor do I mean ally, which is the word that seems to have claimed the A for itself in the alphabet soup. The word I have in mind is actually autism, which is another one of those terms that have entered common parlance in recent times, but that have also been expanded to such a ridiculous extent that they have been rendered almost completely meaningless.

In a nutshell, up until a couple of decades ago the use of that particular term was almost entirely restricted to the most severe cases, the ones in which the condition is truly crippling, and prevents those who have it from becoming fully functioning members of society. In fact up until 2013 Asperger syndrome, which is now included within the context of the autistic spectrum, was treated as an entirely separate diagnosis. Now, as happens to be the case with most of the things we are talking about in this book, what we are referring to here is a label, and one that can be applied in a somewhat arbitrary fashion. It is a condition that can only be identified by its symptoms, and other external manifestations, and while there is no denying the fact that in the most serious of cases —those that have always been recognized— we are most definitely talking about a medical condition that warrants that particular designation, by expanding it to cover such a wide spectrum without making a clear distinction what we have created is a problem, especially because there are laws in the books in a number of areas (for instance when it comes to issues such as immigration, where countries have a right to pick and choose the people they want, and anti-discrimination laws often offer no protection) that, taking that outdated definition as their starting point, classify the milder 'cases' as disabled, and even severely disabled, when nothing could be further from the truth. In fact some of the people who are now considered to be 'on the spectrum' are about as disabled as homosexuals have always been. After all, it wasn't that long ago that that one too was classified as a form of mental illness.

Of course, here it is the lumping together of severe and mild cases, of high and low functioning autism, with the ones who were previously deemed to have Asperger's being thrown in for good measure, under a single heading that doesn't necessarily make sense. The spectrum has grown so broad as to encompass pretty much everyone. In addition to that we have what I suspect is a rather significant cohort that has either fallen through the cracks, or who have been lucky enough to escape a truly monumental display of stupidity that would have seen them labeled for life, depending on how you see the current definition. The reason? Because for the most part the fact that autism is diagnosed when children are of school age, and given the shifting definition, and the continued broadening of the spectrum (plus the growing awareness that autism is *not* restricted to the most extreme cases among both parents and teachers), means that the older you are, the less likely you are to have been tagged as having 'high functioning autism' in your early days happens to be. Again whether that is a blessing or a curse is open for debate. And what does that have to do with anything (or at least with the subject at hand)?

It has to do with the fact that, at least going by the few tentatives studies that have been done on the subject, asexuality seems to be far more prevalent among those who are deemed to be on the spectrum than among the general population... and in a way that makes sense because while autism is effectively treated as a pathology, and asexuality is not, at the end of the day they do share a critical feature, namely the fact that they both refer to a large extent to the way in which a given individual interacts with those around them, and whether or not those interactions fall within the scope of what would be described as 'normal' by society at large (and while only one of them is formally described as a 'condition', in both of those cases society's answer seems to be a resounding 'no').

In fact another word we often see used to refer to those who are on the spectrum is 'neuroatypical'. It is, or rather was, a good word, unfortunately it is also another one of those umbrella terms that seemed sensible enough in the beginning, but it is also one that by now has been borrowed by so many people, and put to so many utterly unrelated uses, that it has been rendered almost completely meaningless, as the number of 'conditions' it supposedly covers keeps expanding on a seemingly daily basis.

At first it referred primarily to those on the autistic spectrum, but usually excluded the most severe cases, which as I mentioned above was a sensible distinction. It was a word that was readily understandable, it sounded friendlier, and it also went a long way towards avoiding the stigma and pathologization that had traditionally been associated with the term 'autism', but then other conditions were added to the mix. These were, for the most part (or at least officially) those conditions that were undeniably real, but at the same time couldn't be diagnosed via a blood test or a brain scan, meaning that diagnosing them could be more art than science, especially around the edges. By that I mean things such as ADHD, OCD, eating disorders, anxiety issues, and the like, i.e. conditions that describe behaviors that don't quite fit the norm —including some that can be harmful, and even life-threatening— but that don't represent a developmental delay, or any form of learning disability (though dyslexia is sometimes included, a fact that only serves to further muck things up in that regard). The end result? That the word was reduced, at least in some circles, to being yet another well-meaning attempt to change the words in an effort to shift the way we speak without really changing our minds and attitudes, or at least some minds and attitudes, enough of them to remain a problem, but back to our story. To the origins of the term, when it referred primarily to those who are on the autistic spectrum.

The thing is that the term neuroatypical, at least when we go by its most literal interpretation (meaning those whose thought processes fall outside the norms of society without being disabled), can be seen to include asexuality itself, though it is important to know that, while asexuality seems to be particularly prevalent among those who are said to be on the spectrum, the opposite does not hold true. That the vast majority of people on that autistic spectrum are *not* asexual, and in fact their inability to express their sexuality in a 'normal', or at least socially acceptable fashion, is one of the most challenging issues parents with children on said spectrum have to deal with... and the fact that the definition of autism keeps changing, that it keeps expanding to engulf other terms that have not always fallen under that particular umbrella means that we may reach a point where asexuality will come to be seen, if not as a form of autism, at least as a possible symptom of it. That would make mainstream, or neurotypical, society, far more comfortable... and at the end of the day there is very little we can do to prevent that. Now, for the time being, when the world seems to be fascinated by the concept of autism, and there is a concerted effort to destigmatize at least the milder cases, to even paint the condition in an unrealistic, and ridiculously favorable light, that wouldn't necessarily be such a big deal.

In fact that destigmatization effort has given rise to a phenomenon in which we have an ever growing number of adults that were never diagnosed as children (remember that cohort I mentioned above who had either been spared, or fallen through the cracks, depending on your point of view?), who are now going back, and getting the diagnosis they had originally escaped in an attempt to find an explanation for what they perceive to be their own awkwardness. This is not necessarily a bad thing, as that diagnosis can enable them to access a number of resources, services and protections that would otherwise be beyond their reach, and that can make it easier for them to function in the big, bad world, but I fear that just as the pendulum swung one way (away from that stigmatization), it may eventually do so in the opposite direction, and if we ever come to that point those who are now seeking that explanation, those who take comfort on the fact that they now have an official name they can use almost as a shield, may find themselves stuck with a label that cannot be easily removed... and that in turn is why I dread the possibility that asexuality may someday come to be seen as a possible indicator of autism, even if it is not likely to ever be fully equated with such a diagnosis.

8. Friend Is Not a Dirty Word

As far as I can tell there are few things men fear as much as being chucked into the dreaded 'friendzone', you know, where women treat them as friends. Yes, I know, the horror! Okay, so I also realize that this is not a universal concern, that the friendzone is a construct that comes into play only in those instances in which the men (and it is usually the men, or maybe that is just my experience as a woman) want a different kind of relationship than the one they are being offered (which, when they are dealing with an asexual woman, is something like 99.9% of the time), and they get rebuffed.

To put it bluntly, straight men seem to be absolutely convinced that a) they are utterly irresistible, b) they are actually being nice to me, so how can I treat them so callously, and fail to reciprocate their advances, and c) that as far as they are concerned friendship is (almost) never enough. Of course all women lust after their bodies, and if we don't, well, then there's got to be something wrong with us, right? This, unfortunately, is an attitude I have come across more times than I care to remember, even when I make it absolutely clear from the start that, no, I am most definitely not interested; that that is never going to change; that I will never be interested; that they are not my cup of tea (or coffee, or even hot chocolate). It is also true even though I am at an age when hormones are supposed to have settled down a bit, so maybe men can start thinking with the heads that are actually on their shoulders.

Okay, so maybe things *have* gotten a little better in that regard, but the tension remains. I am a single woman, and therefore I am supposed to find them irresistible. That is the natural order of things (or so they think). That tends to make interactions more than a little awkward, as I keep waiting for the other shoe to drop. Oh, and as if that weren't enough, there is also the fact that that is not the extent of the problem because even in those instances in which the men themselves don't take offense due to my clear lack of interest in anything more than friendship, their girlfriends/wives/SOs are often a different story. They are wary, they are suspicious, and that problem is even worse when the man in question happens to be the boyfriend/husband/SO of one of my own friends.

In a nutshell, even if I make it absolutely clear that I am most definitely *not* interested, that there is nothing going on, and that there will never be anything going on because, wonderful as they may be, as far as I'm concerned their partners are not my freaking cup of tea, more often than not they seem to be unable to grasp that fact. They too seem to be unable to wrap their minds around the notion that I don't find the partners they are so gleefully showing off utterly irresistible.

It has gotten to the point that I dread the very notion of having my friends introduce me to their partners at all, because I may not be interested in those partners, but I do value those friendships, and as far as I am concerned those introductions are a minefield I would much rather do without.

Okay, so I admit that I have finally come to a point in my life where that is no longer as much of an issue as it once was. That for the most part my friends' relationships are now pretty stable, so those introductions are becoming increasingly rare, not to mention that by now the friends I still have have long since figured out that when I say I'm not interested, I truly mean I'm not interested, so fresh bouts of jealousy are unlikely (and the fact that now I *do* have a label I can use to explain my disinterest doesn't exactly hurt matters), but there was a time when I felt like I was in some sort of a demolition derby, one that wound up costing me countless friendships of the kind that cannot be easily replaced. You can't make new lifelong friends when you are in your thirties and forties, that is not how the system works, and the older you get, the fewer the shared experiences you are bound to have with whatever new friends you happen to make.

As for men thinking they are irresistible? Nope, that doesn't look like it's going to be changing any time soon, or ever.

That is one of the main reasons why I keep saying that being asexual is something that can at times feel incredibly isolating, and the most annoying aspect of the whole thing is that there really is no need for it to be. It is just a byproduct of others' expectations, of their inability to even begin to comprehend what being asexual actually entails. They are operating and reacting in fear based on the standard set of societal expectations, while we are pretty far removed from it.

In fact I suspect this is worse for those of us who are asexual than for those who identify as either gay or lesbian. Yes, gays and lesbians too are operating out of what are the traditionally defined bounds of society, they are also out of what are the most traditional expectations, but at least they can point to something that comes across as a viable alternative. They can point to a competing set of interests that can be seen as superseding the more traditional ones in their minds, and that is something that society *can* accept... or at least recognize. In fact it is not uncommon for them to be able to point to the existence of an actual partner. For most of us that is not an option.

You want to know a little secret? We may not be interested in sex, some of us may not even be interested in romance (not to mention that finding a partner who is interested in romance, but is willing to go without sex... well, that is not exactly easy), but in spite of that we are still human, we are still social beings, and we still crave friendship and companionship, but while for the most part we don't see our asexuality as our primary defining characteristic (not in the way gay, lesbian, and trans individuals seem to do), there is no getting around the fact that, because of other people's expectations and reactions, more often than not we wind up cut off from the rest of the world. That trying to find someone who actually understands, and accepts where we are coming from, when that from seems so alien to them, can be all but impossible, but in spite of that the need is still there, and it is still going unmet.

It is the nature of the game, of the way we play it, or maybe it is a consequence of the fact that we refuse to play it at all.

9. If It Ain't Broke Don't Fix It

In a previous chapter I mentioned that one of the things that have changed over the course of the past few decades is that asexuality seems to be moving against the grain as it gains a wider and wider prominence. That while homosexuality and gender dysphoria have been officially removed from the list of mental illnesses, asexuality has gone from being so invisible that it wasn't even acknowledged, to being seen as a problem, something that must be addressed, something that must be fixed.

I remember a fairly obscure book I read a long time ago: Fredric Brown's 1955 *Martians, Go Home* (and please note that I *do* mean the book. There is a movie out there. I think it dates back to 1990, or something like that. Do *not* watch the movie! It is one of those movies that will make you feel an instinctive need to get up and leave, never to return, only chances are you will be watching it at home because no self respecting theater would show it ever again. That will do nothing to quell your instinctive desire to escape, to run away. Still, it is not the book's fault, and while the book in question is not one of the greatest literary masterpieces ever written, it can be enjoyable enough if it catches you in the right frame of mind, but I run the risk of losing the plot here, so let's try to get this train wreck back on track). In that book the martians show up, and yes, they are indeed little green men from Mars. They are not violent, in fact they are, for all intents and purposes, non-corporeal, they just... tell the truth. They see everything, they hear everything, and they say everything. You can imagine how well human society fares in their presence. The truth, the whole truth, and nothing but the truth? It just can't cope. That is not a kind of situation we are equipped to handle. Anyway, and without going into too much detail, just in case you want to read it, at one point the protagonist loses the 'ability' to see and hear the martians. He is at peace, he is not bothered by their absence (or their presence), though he realizes everyone else is convinced that the martians are real, that they are actually there. He winds up in a mental institution, and the psychologists are wondering how to treat him, or even if they should treat him at all. He is content while everyone else is miserable, is that something that should be *fixed*? That is the most obvious connection of the plot with the current tendency to treat asexuality as a form of sexual dysfunction, but oddly enough this book offers us not one, but rather two analogies. Yes, we are like the man in the insane asylum who is perfectly content *not* seeing the martians, even as said martians drive everyone else up the wall, but we are also like the martians themselves, who see everything from the outside, including the way in which sexuality complicates people's lives (in fact, as far as they are concerned, sex is absolutely hilarious), and they have no qualms about pointing it out.

What can I say? Maybe something along the lines of 'I can relate'? Yups, that about sums it up. I don't get sex, and to most people the very notion that I don't get it is what is all but impossible to comprehend. They think I'm broken, I think they are crazy. That is not a good starting point if we want to come to some sort of an understanding.

Of course, being asexual in the current climate is not always easy (okay, so maybe it wasn't exactly easy in the past either, when we didn't even have a term that was readily available we could use to define ourselves, and all we knew was that our responses were fundamentally different from the ones of those around us; when we truly thought we were broken because... well, what else could we be?). We are excluded and misunderstood; we have a hard time fitting in; we can't even come out right because... well, because we remain mostly a puzzle, though to be fair I suspect that is a problem that cuts both ways. Sexuality too can seem all but incomprehensible to us at times, it's just that we have had it shoved down our throats since the day we were born, so we have sort of learned to navigate that world, a world where the lives others lead seem twisted and distorted to us, just as our own lives seem to them. We don't need to be 'cured' of something you deem to be a problem. We are who we are, we are not broken, we don't have to be fixed, we don't have to be made to see the martians just so that we can be as miserable as everyone else.

Oh, I know that's not how most people see it, and honestly, there is a ton of crap I just don't want to have to deal with, that is why up until now I have kept a low profile, and hardly ever spoken about this with anyone (though I have grown more and more comfortable with the label as the years go by. It is not something that happened overnight).

Besides, it's not like it matters, or rather it's not like it matters much. Shockingly I can go about my life without having sex, without obsessing about having sex, or about the sex I'm *not* having. I'm not jumping from one disastrous relationship to the next for fear of being alone, and as far as I'm concerned that has to count for something.

Let me put it another way, one you will hopefully find more relatable: I am a self-confessed chocoholic, but I don't think there's something wrong with not liking chocolate. In fact I do realize that, inconceivable as the notion may seem from my perspective, there are plenty of people out there who can't stand the stuff. Does that make sense to me? Not really, but then again I realize that it's none of my business. They are well within their right not to like it, and the fact that they don't doesn't mean that there is something fundamentally wrong with them. There are just no rules in that regard.

10. Growing Up Is Hard to Do

Yes, I know it may sound unbelievable by the standards of the generations that have come of age in the current millennium, but as I've mentioned before, I was something like thirty years old by the time the word asexual first entered my vocabulary, by the time I finally found a term I could use to describe what had been my personal experience up to that point. The thing is that back in the Dark Ages, before the internet came along in the mid-nineties, our access to information was extremely limited, and even over the course of the first few years of its existence the subject was not one that was ever even mentioned, so I had no real reason to go looking for it. I had no reason to believe such a term even existed. As far as I knew I was just me, weird, but me... and that in turn helped make what were my already awkward teenage years even more awkward, something I suspect is more common than those who are *not* asexual can even begin to comprehend.

It was only twenty years ago, in 2001, that AVEN (Asexual Visibility and Education Network, one of the most prominent asexual online communities) was founded.

Anyway, the point is that back when I was in high school most of my classmates were going out on dates, going to parties, falling in and out of looove, flirting, and buying way too many clothes, while my mom... I think my mom felt like the only mom in the whole world who regularly found herself begging her teenage daughter to please, *please*, *PLEASE* at least *look* at some clothes (and she in turn was an intellectual who, while she had a pretty good fashion sense if the need arose, would probably have rated 'shopping' as one of her least favorite activities). As for me... well, I was, and still am, perfectly content with a pair of jeans and a t-shirt (preferably an oversized one). As for boys pestering me, socializing, and going to parties? That was the last thing I wanted to have to deal with. In fact for the most part I just wanted my 'peers' to buzz off.

My parents believed that I was shy and socially awkward, which I was. I was the ultimate outsider, but I guess they assumed it was just a quirk, or maybe I was a lesbian, but wasn't ready to admit it, not even to myself, or... well, you get the general idea.

High school was bad in that regard, and college was not much better. My saving grace when it came to that one was that I decided *not* to go away to college, but chose to keep living at home instead. The truth is that I don't think I could have survived what passed for dorm life, especially not in the late eighties and early nineties. I just wanted to be left alone, and living with my parents gave me the opportunity to do just that.

Was it just the asexuality thing? I'm not sure, and chances are I'll never be. It is true that I was never particularly sociable, that I was never popular (in fact I was bullied, and bullied relentlessly, due to a number of other issues ever since I can remember), and to this day I have trouble fitting in, an issue that can't really be pinned on this particular label, but it certainly didn't help matters.

Once the internet came along it made it easier for me to make sense of what was going on. My access to information was no longer limited to the books and resources that were physically available in my location, or to the subjects those in my immediate vicinity were willing, or able, to talk about.

As I said, that is one thing that sets us old geezers apart from the younger generation.

Yes, it may seem obvious in hindsight, but well, you know what they say about that, and kids today will never know that particular struggle. They will never know what it means to go through their teens and twenties wondering what the heck is going on, what is 'wrong' with them... knowing that they are different, seeing the way people interact, and just scratching their heads because, honestly, none of it seems to make sense (and yes, I know I am beginning to sound like a cantankerous old woman, but that is yet another label I am slowly learning to embrace because, as much as things have improved in some aspects, there are other areas in which I fear we may actually be going backwards).

Ace spaces are still few and far between, but there are a few, mostly virtual, ones that are beginning to emerge. Awareness may be lagging, and there may still be those who are trying to pathologize us, and see us as defective, as broken somehow, but there is also a growing awareness out there. The information is finally available (at least to those who bother to go looking for it), and they don't even have to look too hard to find it... though asexuality may still be isolating. It all depends on where you are (and where on the ace spectrum you happen to fall).

Sure, if you live in a major city chances are that you will find someone. If you live in a small town? Well, there things can get tricky. Let's say your town has a population of 20,000, and that maybe one percent of those are somewhere on the ace spectrum. That means that there are maybe two hundred people that fall into this particular category. That doesn't sound too bad, but that may be cut in half if you feel more affinity towards men or towards women, if you are either hetero or homoromantic. So let's say we are down to one hundred, but that is across all the age spectrum (and not excluding those who are aromantic, or maybe you are aromantic yourself, which would take the homoromantic, heteroromantic and biromantic members of your local community out of the equation), so maybe there are ten people who are within striking distance of your own age group, and two thirds of those are likely to be too far away from you on the *ace* spectrum for a relationship to be a real possibility. Now pick three people at random. What are the chances that anything remotely resembling your so-called 'true soulmate' (or even someone with whom you can conceivably establish something remotely resembling a healthy, long-term relationship) will be found within that lot? Not too good I guess (after all our asexuality is just one of the countless aspects that help make us who we are), and that is not even considering the percentage that may be oblivious to what they are, so the real number may drop to one or two... if you are lucky.

Of course, I also realize that this is a problem that is not restricted to those on the ace spectrum, that it also affects the rest of the LGBTQ+ community, and to a certain extent even those who are straight: your dating pool is, more often than not, determined by your location. It is a matter of chance, and even though dating apps, and especially social media, have made it easier for us to connect with those who are near us, but don't belong to our inner circle... well, the problem remains unresolved. After all, what we are talking about here is a kind of relationship where proximity matters, and those numbers are most definitely an issue (that, and that in quite a few instances those dating apps don't even list asexuality as an option, rendering them effectively useless).

If there is one thing the pandemic has taught us it is that while technology has made it possible for us to connect in ways that would have been unthinkable only a couple of decades ago, Zoom romances are not, and will probably never be, a thing, meaning that the limited number of people who actually identify as asexual in our immediate vicinity is bound to remain an issue for the foreseeable future, and that, that is something we are going to have no choice but to deal with.

11. Intersections

There is a cover of John Lennon's *Imagine* by the a cappella group Pentatonix. It is well worth listening to, but of course, that is not what makes it relevant here. What makes it relevant is the fact that there is a point in the video where one of the members picks up a piece of cardboard, and on it he writes the letters LGBTQ+, then he hands that sign to the next member. That second member flips it over, and we see the word 'man' written there. The sign is then passed on to the third member, who flips it over first to the word 'Jewish', and then to the word 'American'. After that he hands it over to the fourth member. He takes the sign, and flips it to 'Black', and then to 'Christian'. Then the sign is passed on to the final member of the group. She takes the word 'Christian', and flips it first to 'Latina', and finally to 'woman'. It is a very touching display about the labels we all carry, and also about how those labels both bring us together, and set us apart, as each of those labels does indeed apply to the corresponding member of that group. We can argue about how relevant each of those happens to be, but at the end of the day they not only serve to define us in our own minds, but they also have a major impact on how we are perceived by those around us. Granted, some are more visible/relevant than others, and at the end of the day there is no getting around the fact that not all labels are equally apparent, but they are most definitely there, part of the baggage we carry.

Black or white? Those are usually pretty apparent, or at least they are supposed to be, but clear cut as those words may make the distinction sound from a distance, the closer we look, the blurrier they become because at the end of the day the situation is far more nuanced than those two words would seem to suggest. Simply put, there are way more than two choices here, not to mention that biracial, and multiracial, people are anything but unheard of, so that whole black or white thing? It is a shorthand at best. Man or woman? Well, those two would seem to offer a more obvious dichotomy, at least at first glance. The problem is that, just as was the case in the previous instance, that first glance can, and often does, get us in trouble, especially nowadays when a growing number of people are rejecting those labels outright, and I don't just mean people who identify as trans, hence the rise in the use of they/their pronouns (and the resulting controversy between those who demand that their choice be respected, those who object to it as a matter of principle, and those who object to it because of grammar, and the fact that to their ears the whole thing sounds like nails on a chalkboard, even though the form has been used, albeit in a far more limited fashion, for a very long time). Jewish, Christian, Muslim, and the like? Well, there you basically have to ask. It is not something that is immediately apparent, not unless the person in question chooses to make a blatant display of that label by their choice of attire, or something along those lines, and for the most part the same holds true when it comes to sexual orientation.

In my case 'asexual' is one of the labels I carry, along with 'woman', 'Latina', 'Jewish' (okay, so that one is kind of iffy because at the end of the day I am so far from being a practicing Jew that it's not even funny, and neither were my parents, but for whatever reason that is the one religious label society has deemed a hereditary trait... blame it on a long history of antisemitism, especially in Europe, and on the assumption that the 'taint' is in our blood, but more on that later), and 'immigrant'. So how do I see those five labels?

'Woman', or maybe I should say 'female', is the easiest one of the lot. It is a label that was assigned to me on the day I was born. It is on my birth certificate, and it defines how the world at large sees me. In fact it is the first thing anyone notices about me (let's face it, we live in a world where, when a baby is born, the first thing people ask, even before 'is it healthy?' is 'is it a boy or a girl?', or at least that was the case before the advent of ultrasounds rid us of the unbearable element of surprise when it comes to that one, and replaced it with things such as gender reveal parties. That is how relevant that question is deemed to be by society at large), and while for the most part I have no problem with it (nor do I have a problem equating 'woman' with 'female' in my particular case, and I do find both labels equally acceptable), I do realize that there are others who are not so lucky; that precisely because it is so critical, a misidentification when it comes to this most fundamental of labels can be absolutely devastating. 'Latina'? Well, yes, I am most definitely one, at least for a certain value of it, and I am proud of that fact, but I don't really fit the stereotype (blame it on the next one of those labels, because even though most government forms in the United States have a checkbox labeled 'non-Hispanic Jew', the fact is that while my forefathers did originally emigrate to South America, they were German, Russian, Romanian, and the like so no, 'Latina' is not the first word that is likely to come to anyone's mind when they see me). As I mentioned before, the label 'Jewish' doesn't make sense, not when it comes to my beliefs, which are what it is supposed to reflect, but it is there, and because of my name I have had some mild, but still unpleasant, brushes with antisemitism, enough to make me angry, enough to make me defensive. If you treat it like a mark of shame, I will pick it as a badge of honor. It is a natural reaction, so even though I don't think it really represents me, I am not itching to shed it. I may not think of myself as Jewish, but I do realize that that is how some people perceive me, and while some of the assumptions with regards to my world view that tend to go with that particular label really, *really*, REALLY bug me, I know they are part of a package, that I don't get to pick and choose, not when it comes to how others see me... and the extent to which that particular label *doesn't* fit is also a good indicator as to the limits of those labels when it comes to defining us. Those three are the big ones I got stuck with just by virtue of being born, and then there are the other two (okay, so there are way more than two, but those are by far the most relevant ones), that I picked somewhere along the way.

The first one of those is 'Immigrant', and that is one that, just like 'woman', can be readily apparent, at least in some instances, and the second one is 'asexual', which is once more an utterly invisible label. Like the other three, neither one of these labels refers to something that was actually my choice. One is derived from a significant event in my early childhood (the fact that my parents had to flee my home country when I was five. In fact that label could just as easily have been 'refugee' rather than 'immigrant', but my parents applied for residence, not asylum, so 'immigrant' I became, and that in turn shows how tenuous the distinction between some of these labels can actually be), and the second one is 'asexual', which is what this book is all about, and it is one I may well have been born with, but that just wasn't apparent at the time. As far as Venn diagrams go, the resulting one is pretty complicated, so much so that it can't be fully represented on paper, but that is not exactly surprising. It is also, at the end of the day, a fairly inaccurate picture of this particular Dalmatian, one that ignores a gazillion minor labels that I carry, labels I may pick up or shed depending on the circumstances, and on who is doing the labeling (things such as 'friend', 'daughter', 'cousin', 'progressive', 'loner', 'weirdo', 'moron', and so on). Yes, I exist at the intersection of all those labels, both major and minor, public and private, friendly and unfriendly, but at the same time I am more than a mere collection of these tags, and the same holds true for each and every one of us. But let's get back to the subject of this book, and focus on how the label 'asexual' interacts with the rest of the lot.

In a way this is related to something I mentioned in the *Shades of Grey* chapter: even if we share one specific label, at the end of the day we are all individuals, and the way in which we experience that particular label often varies, or is affected by the other labels we carry, be it the ones we choose, or the ones others assign to us. My experience with regards to the term 'asexual' as a woman is probably quite different from what a man's would be, and the other labels I carry are also likely to play a role when it comes to that. The extent to which that difference can be traced to those other labels, or to my own experiences and personality, is all but impossible to determine, just as it is impossible to determine where the demarcating line between those influences should be. There are too many factors, too many variables, too many moving parts, so much so that any attempt at establishing any sort of causal connection is bound to fall flat on its face.

There is a limit to the scientific method in that regard, and human beings are far more complex than an artificially set up experiment, or constrained set of observations, can possibly hope to describe.

Take one of the labels I do have something of an issue with: 'Jewish'. As I said, it does not represent my religious beliefs at all, and as a woman I am not too keen on being associated with a religion in which men have traditionally prayed on a daily basis to thank God for not having made them women, but at the same time it is also a label that is indelibly associated with my name. As an immigrant, and almost a refugee, I am not too keen on Israel's treatment of the Palestinians (and the fact that people can't seem to tell the difference between Jewish and Zionist doesn't exactly help matters here because the second one is a label I *do* reject outright, one that most definitely doesn't fit, but that fuels a great deal of the antisemitism we see in the world today, antisemitism I have experienced myself, meaning that no matter how I feel about it, I can't quite escape it). On the other hand, 'Jewish' is a label that connects me with my family, with my past. It is also a label that reflects a cultural tradition that, with its emphasis on educational achievement, did shape my life to a significant extent, even if it did so indirectly, and I wasn't always aware of its influence. In other words, it is a label that connects me to a long tradition that, for all its flaws, has plenty of elements I am more than happy to embrace.

As for the label 'asexual' itself, that one is like a Russian nesting doll, with a number of sub-labels attached that try to further define it. That is something I touched on in a previous chapter, and yet these are sub-labels I hesitate to embrace for a number of reasons. One of them is the fact that for the most part I feel that labels as a whole are a little too inflexible to provide much nuance, so while they can come in handy when trying to paint a general picture, they can also get us into trouble because we ourselves are not immutable. In addition to that there is also the fact that at the end of the day we all see the world from our own perspectives, and there are too many instances in which I fear that any attempt at defining them may lead to some confusion because we can't truly explain what we actually mean, and we can easily end up assigning different names to a single position, or a single name to two positions that are fundamentally different. Is teal a shade of blue or of green? Asexual is easy enough, there are no shades of grey when it comes to that one in my particular case, or almost, or maybe I should say I don't think there are (again I can only speak to my own experience, and that makes it impossible for me to compare it to that of others), but other than that I would say I am probably panromantic, leaning towards homoromantic, but also bordering on aromantic, and moderately sex repulsed, though what that 'moderately' means, or where it truly stands on that particular spectrum, well, when it comes to that one I am still basically drawing a blank. Clear as mud, right? See, I told you there was a reason I was reluctant to embrace these sub-labels.

The thing is that that mix of tags is the one that defines me, at least in the eyes of the world at large. It is what makes me unique, but at the same time I am no more unique than anyone else because at the end of the day we all carry our own labels, and we exist at our own intersections. We all see the world from our own perspective, sexual or asexual, straight, gay, bi, or trans, so let me close this chapter by going right back to where I started: to the video of Pentatonix's cover of John Lennon's *Imagine*. That one ends with each member of the group picking up a blank piece of cardboard. We see them writing on them, and when they are done they flip them over, revealing a single letter on each sign. Together those letters form the word 'human', which at the end of the day is the only label that truly matters.

12. More Than Meets the Eye

In a way this book is all about labels, or at least about one particular label, and while in the previous chapter I sort of hinted at what I perceive to be the limitations of that concept, in this one I am going to be tackling those head on.

For starters I want to go back to the crux of this book, and of my own experience: the fact that it took a while for me to even find a label that could even begin to describe my own experience, one that actually fit, but while the fact that I didn't have a term I could use to define myself did have some important downsides when it came to my ability to figure out just what was 'wrong' with me, I also belong to a generation that, for the most part, tended to see being labeled as a dirty word... and I freely admit that that rejection of that particular concept colors my perceptions to this day. See for instance how I view my relationship with the terms 'Jewish' and 'Latina' I mentioned in the previous chapter. In fact those are words that, up until I wrote this book, I had hardly ever mentioned in connection to myself, and with a little luck once this thing is published I will also be free to send them back to the back burner, where they belong. I am me, and that is how I want to be perceived, and even though I am willing to admit that at times some labels *can* come in handy, for the most part I tend to find them too narrow, too confining.

The younger generation, and the LGBTQ+ community, on the other hand, seem to be obsessed with collecting as many of the blasted things as they possibly can, hence the number of shades of grey and sub-labels we are supposed to embrace in an attempt to describe just where we fit on that particular spectrum... and some of them also seem to be determined to experiment, to find a label that is *not* cis, heterosexual, and so on that they can use to describe themselves. Being ordinary is boring, and they want to be seen as anything but.

Back when I was growing up the battlecry seemed to be something along the lines of 'don't label me!', now that has morphed into 'label me, but do it without denying my uniqueness... in fact I want those labels to reflect the fact that I am different, that I am totally unlike anyone else!'

In a way I think it is absolutely adorable, in another I wonder if in the end they won't just end up doing themselves more damage in their quest for that unique set of labels than they would have done by eschewing labels altogether (or, worse yet, if the trivialization of those labels, courtesy of kids who want to be seen as edgy, won't end up backfiring on the LGBTQ+ community as a whole, a community that has spent decades fighting for its own legitimacy, and to get rid of the notion that sexual orientation is a matter of choice), but of course, that is not my decision to make, and the fact that experimentation has come to be seen as normal is most definitely a good thing because, at the end of the day, we may all need some time to get our feet under us, to sort out who we actually are.

In fact one of the questions I asked in the *A Is for Ally* chapter was whether the Q in the alphabet soup stands for queer or for questioning, and while for the most part the answer to that one seems to be 'queer', the fact that 'questioning' is seen as a legitimate option is kind of telling, because we have finally come to a place where the notion of experimenting, of not really knowing how we define ourselves from the get go, or which labels, if any, actually apply to us, is at long last being embraced.

The thing is that whether we like them or not, labels matter. They help us make sense of the world around us by keeping us from getting lost in the details, and they help us understand how the world sees us in turn, not to mention that we humans have an almost instinctive need to classify... well, to classify pretty much everything, to tell you the truth, and yes, that does include other humans. In fact humans are one of the things we spend most time trying to lump into easily defined categories, but at the same time we are all almost painfully aware of the fact that we ourselves are more than a mere collection of labels. It is a balance that can be all but impossible to maintain. We are all individuals, and the labels the world insists on attaching to us in order to put us in a neat little box, to make sense out of us, can at times feel a little too narrow, and too restrictive for comfort... and yet, as I found out the hard way as I was trying to make some sort of sense out of my own asexuality, their absence can be just as devastating. This is nothing new, in fact the concept can probably be traced all the way back to Plato, with his theory of Forms or Ideas, where basically the Forms (or what we would call labels) are what is real. They depict the true essence of things, and everything else is dismissed as an illusion.

Okay, so the whole theory is a good deal more complicated than that, and this is not a treatise on philosophy, so that's about as deep as we are going to go into that one, but the thing is that our minds have an almost instinctive tendency to label things, to classify everything. To focus on commonalities to keep from being overwhelmed, but when we do that we inevitably lose sight of the details, so we keep adding more and more labels in an attempt to get those details back into focus, in an attempt to narrow things down, and that is where this whole thing tends to get (even more) complicated. It is where we get to the point where we may just be better off saying 'no' to labels altogether, not that that is particularly feasible.

That's just not the way we are wired.

It is an interesting dichotomy, one that manifests itself in a number of places, but also one that has, to a large extent, been brought to the fore by this newfound determination of ours to define our sexuality and our gender identity in what is, for the most part, a new fashion. They have morphed into a way to codify our individuality in terms others can more readily understand, or at least that is the theory. Instead of eschewing labels we are coming to see ourselves as increasingly complicated Venn diagrams of overlapping identities, but as those diagrams grow more and more complex they are also turning into a sort of cubist painting, one that attempts to capture the model from different angles at the same time, and we wind up turning ourselves into something that looks utterly unrecognizable in the process.

We are who we are, and yes, we may look different when seen from different perspectives, but even though our attempts to capture those different perspectives in a single frame are bound to fall flat on their faces, that doesn't mean we are not ourselves, that we are not more than the sum of those labels (or the resulting bundle of contradictions), so yes, labels can come in handy, but it helps to keep in mind that at the end of the day they are just labels, and that while roadsigns may be incredibly useful when it comes to helping us get a general idea of what lies ahead, they are not the road, they do not represent the path we need to traverse, nor do they represent our final destination.

13. Invisible Means

Well, at least we'll always have Sherlock Holmes... or we will if the gay community doesn't manage to wrestle him away.

What can I say, the depictions of asexuality in film and literature are few and far between, and the few that are out there are not exactly flattering... and in a way I get it. I get that just as I don't get sex, those who are *not* asexual just can't seem to wrap their minds around the notion of asexuality, and there are more of them out there than there are of us, so they are usually the ones doing the writing. Add to that the fact that up until some twenty years ago the word wasn't even in common use (and even today it is far less prevalent than the rest of the terms that make up the alphabet soup), and what you get is not so much a deliberate attempt to silence the ace position, but rather something that looks like it, but is not quite as deliberate... or at least that was the case up until fairly recently, because the truth is that that is beginning to change, and not necessarily for the better.

In the current climate a negative depiction of a gay or trans character would be met with outrage. It would be condemned as a matter of principle. A negative depiction of an ace character? Well, that one will be met at most with a shrug. In fact in those rare instances in which asexuality is openly depicted, it is usually treated either as a lifestyle choice, or as a problem that must be addressed. It is still depicted as something that is, at the end of the day, unnatural. It is something that must be fixed, and one of the tropes is the storyline in which the seemingly asexual individual winds up falling in love (in other words, these stories have, as their culmination, a scenario in which a previously asexual character yields to society's expectations, and end with the traditional 'and they lived happily ever after', a.k.a. 'and then they f*cked', which is something I find incredibly annoying).

No, we have never encountered the levels of hostility and institutionalized discrimination that have met other orientations until ridiculously recently, and that in turn is likely to have played a not insignificant role in our own lack of awareness and organization. It was women who took the lead in the fight for women's rights at a time when the law treated them as little more than children, and it was gays and lesbians (and eventually trans) individuals who led the fight to pass anti-discrimination legislation, and one of the reasons they did that was... well, because it was actually necessary, because they had some skin in the game. They did it because they were not just ignored, but rather actively rejected. They did it because there were laws in the books that penalized homosexuality (especially among men). They did it because their very essence was described as a disease. They were not just invisible, not like we are, but rather they were actively persecuted. When we think of the holocaust we think primarily of the six million Jews, but there were also tens of thousands of homosexuals who shared their fate, to say nothing of those who were subjected to all sorts of 'medical experiments' as the nazi's sought a 'cure'. These, together with the Roma people, are the forgotten victims of the holocaust, the ones that continued (and in some cases continue) to be persecuted by mainstream society long after the camps themselves had been liberated.

As for asexuality, that one just goes unacknowledged both in art and in everyday life, as it has done since time immemorial. Now, this doesn't necessarily mean that there are no characters out there that could probably be described as asexual, as there are plenty of characters out there that are not sexually active... at least not on screen (or on the page). In fact in quite a few genres sexual activity was not even mentioned up until fairly recently. It is just that as long as that was the case, heterosexuality was assumed. That has most definitely changed (Dumbledore, for instance, has been described as gay by J.K. Rowling herself, though there are few, if any, indications of that fact sprinkled throughout the Harry Potter books... okay, so maybe, if you squint hard enough, there are some hints in book seven).

So, are there other major characters that, looking back, would probably qualify as asexual, and not just as not openly sexual, even if they are not officially identified as such? It is hard to tell. When it comes to books and films we only see what writers and directors choose to show us, and there are plenty of characters that are left in limbo in that regard, but personally I would argue that another major character in an important franchise that could reasonably be described as asexual would be Havelock Vetinari, the Machiavellian patrician of

Ankh-Morpork in Terry Pratchett's *Discworld* universe. No, he is not a title character, not in the way Sherlock Holmes is, but he *is* one of the most prominent ones, and given that for the most part the sexuality of the other characters in that series is fairly explicit, I don't think this is just an oversight, but rather something deliberate. Nanny Ogg, for instance, says that 'she herself had had many husbands, and had even been married to three of them'; the wizards are supposed to be celibate; Sam Vimes is married; Carrot is together with someone of a different species (werewolf); and then we have either feminism, or the gay rights movement itself, reflected in the anti-equality struggle of female dwarfs who want to be recognized as such, and not as mere dwarfs. Okay, so the patrician can be cold, and kind of ruthless (understatement of the century), but he is one of the best rulers the city has ever had... besides I said I was looking for asexual, I never said anything about nice (incidentally, if you want nice, minor, and also probably asexual, I would add Leonard da Quirm to the list, but enough about the Disc).

The point is that if we want to find characters that are not an actual sea sponge (yes, I am looking at you SpongeBob SquarePants) that reflect our identity we have to do quite a bit of digging. That, and that even when we do find them, and even in those instances in which they are not depicted in a negative light, nor are they 'fixed' at the end, these characters are still portrayed as different, as cold and calculating, and somehow missing in human empathy. This is true of both Sherlock Holmes and Havelock Vetinari, neither one of whom is a stupid man. In fact they are both geniuses in their own way, but (*The Three Garridebs* and Wuffles notwithstanding), warm and fuzzy is not the first word that comes to mind when we think of either of them.

14. Written by the Alien

As you may have guessed if you are reading these lines, I am a writer (though not necessarily a good one), and while this is a non-fiction, deeply personal account, for the most part I consider myself a fiction writer... one that is really bad at staying on her lane, to be accurate, hence the books on dog care, social issues, language learning, and even music theory, out of all things (no, I'm not the biggest fan of specialization). Anyway, the thing is that, while in the previous chapter I mentioned how we struggle to find anything remotely resembling an accurate portrayal of an asexual character in film and literature because most authors are *not* asexual themselves, this is about the flip side of that particular equation, and the difficulties sexuality presents to me as an asexual author, because at the end of the day that is a pretty major aspect of what passes for the human experience, which is what literature is supposed to reflect in the first place, but at the same time it is also one that feels totally alien to me. Can I use the fact that, in the current climate, an asexual author writing about anything depicting sexuality could be seen as the ultimate form of cultural appropriation, and get a pass on that one? Okay, so I admit that for the most part I do find the current obsession with the whole cultural appropriation thing to be downright ridiculous (to say nothing of the fact that as an author I find it utterly crippling), because it is basically impossible for *anyone* to write anything that has a diverse cast of characters without stepping on someone's toes in that regard (or without producing a work that will inevitably be condemned for its utter lack of diversity). That does pose something of a challenge, but back to the struggles of an asexual writer in a hypersexualized world.

Yes, up until a few decades ago leaving sexuality at the door was perfectly acceptable, it was even expected, but nowadays? Nope, that has become all but impossible... in fact more often than not, you have to bend over backwards to avoid it in a way that actually comes across as natural, and in addition to that there is also the fact that I don't want my asexuality to become my books' defining characteristic, so it is not exactly front and center there either. Yes, historically there is a long tradition of sidestepping the issue, and for the most part that is what I try to do. As I mentioned before, there are some genres I consider my safe spaces, and even though my eschewing of sexuality in my stories may come across as a little weird, or even outdated, it is not exactly unprecedented... and of course, the fact that these are the genres I am most familiar with doesn't exactly hurt matters, though I do tend to gravitate towards what I would describe as 'the unusual end of the spectrum' (a bit that has absolutely nothing to do with my asexuality).

The thing is that while for the most part non-ace writers have a hard time depicting openly asexual characters in a convincing way because those characters are so far removed from their own everyday experience, the opposite is also true. Yes, we have had sexuality shoved down our throats since the day we were born, and for the most part we have learned to function in a world where that is a prominent feature without seeming *too* out of place (after all, it's not like we have much of a choice when it comes to that one, not considering that we can't exactly pack our bags and leave), but it is not our world... or at least it doesn't feel like mine.

Love stories don't come naturally to me, and that goes double (if not triple, or quadruple... or maybe I should say sextuple) for sex scenes so none of my books is ever likely to end with a good, old-fashioned 'and they lived happily ever after' (or, well, you know what I mean). In fact chances are I will never write anything remotely resembling a sex scene, but totally eschewing sex and romance in all characters *without* winding up with an utterly unrelatable story? That too at times feels all but impossible. My saving grace? The fact that while I do not understand sex and romance, I do understand love and affection, and while to me those are two totally different aspects, the fact that for so many people the notion that there can be love without sex or romance (except on a few very specific instances, such as a parent and child bond) is what feels totally alien means that in those instances in which sexuality would be expected, love and affection can often enable me to bridge the gap, and when I do I wonder if I am truly the one who is missing something vital due to my inability to *get* sexuality, or if they are, due to the fact that they seem to be unable to see past it.

15. Sidestepping the Drama

One of the recurring themes in this book has been the fact that there are a number of areas in which asexuality makes you the ultimate outsider. It may not be something that defines us, but it is something that is most definitely there. In a previous chapter I also mentioned how it can be incredibly isolating. It makes it hard to fit in, and that is a situation that has been compounded by the way in which we talk about the subject of sex has changed over the course of the past half century or so. It went from being a taboo subject that was strictly relegated to the background, to being something we barely dared whisper about, to being front and center of pretty much everything.

That means that we asexuals went from sitting unnoticed in the corner, minding our own business, to being unceremoniously kicked out of the room in what felt like the blink of an eye, but of course there is more to it than that. There are also some things that have always been in the background, some things I would describe as rewards, though most of my friends think I'm absolutely insane for seeing it that way.

I refer mainly to the fact that being asexual makes it easy to sidestep a whole lot of what is, at least from my perspective, utterly needless drama.

In a way it is like watching life go by from the outside. I have no boyfriend/girlfriend issues that I have to worry about. I don't have to deal with the chaos exes tend to invite, or with the tangled mess that are friendships after a breakup when there is a common group of friends that must be divided. Yes, divorce is the most public face of this kind of situation, but it is also one that is reasonably organized. There is a contract that must be dissolved in the eyes of the law, and there are courts to help sort things out in that regard. Even custody is usually adjudicated that way, but the question of who gets the friends? Well, there are no external powers that can help sort out that particular aspect of things, and that in turn has always made those splits particularly tricky. They tend to tear friends' groups apart through a sort of war of attrition, as two members of what was previously a close-knit group can no longer even bring themselves to be together in the same room, so one of them departs, often taking those they were closest to with them.

It is a situation that gets awkward fast, and also one that tends to be repeated time and time again until almost nothing of the original group remains, as people peel away a lot faster than new members can truly be added to the mix... I have seen it happen, but again, always from the outside... and don't even get me started on the mess that is affectionately known as co-parenting, or shared custody agreements, when there are children, and plenty of ill will involved. That one is oodles of fun!

So yeah, there is something asexuals are deemed to be missing, and most people, those who know who and what we are, either see us as weird or as broken. We are pitied. We are told that we don't know what we are missing, and we do realize that there may be something there... but from where we (or at least I) stand? Well, from where we stand more often than not it seems like what we are missing is a whole lot of pointless drama, and that is something we can most definitely do without.

It's like that old saying: you cannot miss what you have never known.

If I were to go blind tomorrow I would mourn the loss of the sunsets till the day I died, but if I had been blind from birth I would never realize what I was missing. I would not know what the fuss was all about, so I would have no reason to mourn that loss, and the inability to tell the difference between races —to even begin to understand the concept of racism from that particular perspective, or to judge people based on their physical appearance— would probably come across as a perfectly acceptable trade off, and I do realize that something like that may be going on here, or at least that is how it may seem to most people.

Yes, I get that sex is great, or at least that's what people keep telling me, and there is a closeness in a good and solid relationship that *can* (but more often than not *does not*) come from that, but the jealousy, and the pettiness, and the stress, and the drama, and the suffering I see everywhere as a result? Well, I have to say that, seeing it from the outside, I cannot imagine anything that would make it worth it... and that in turn is one of the things that make *me* seem particularly alien.

It is both a blindspot and a relief.

No, my asexuality does not define me, and contrary to what this series of texts may seem to suggest, it is not something I spend much time thinking about, but it is something that colors my perception of the world around me, just like trauma and past experience do for everyone. We see the world from our own perspective, and those perspectives can be fundamentally different. That is why more often than not we can't seem to agree on basically anything, why we are constantly at each other's throats, and wondering how the other one can be so blind (I am trying to be polite here) not to see the blindingly obvious.

I remember a ridiculously tiny, and totally unrelated incident that happened a little more than a year ago: I was walking down the beach, and I saw that someone had drawn a Venus/female symbol on the sand using sea shells as a writing material (that would be the circle with the cross at the bottom, or ♀). It looked cute, and I even took a picture of it. As I was heading back home, walking in the opposite direction, I came across the same symbol on the sand, only this time around it looked like the *globus cruciger*, also known as 'the orb and cross', which is a circle with a cross on top. Since the earliest days of the Middle Ages (with the first references to it dating back to the fifth century CE, to be accurate), the *globus cruciger* has been used to symbolize the dominion of the Church over the earth (and considering the fact that the symbol uses an orb, and not a pancake, maybe we could use it to get through people's skulls the fact that no,

Columbus was not the first one to realize that the earth was round once and for all, but I digress... sorry, that one is sort of a pet peeve of mine). Now, I do realize that in the modern world chances are that whoever drew that symbol was going for the Venus sign, that the orb and cross is not a symbol we are likely to come across that often in this day and age, and that chances are that whoever put that thing together wasn't even aware of its existence, but still, as long as you knew them both, which one you saw depended mostly on which way you happened to be going. It encapsulated in an incredibly simple fashion how something that may seem obvious to us may also look completely different to someone who is approaching it from a different angle.

But back to our story. The point I was trying to make is that we all see the world from our perspective. It is something that is too deeply ingrained, and we have a hard time letting go of our preconceived notions, of the things we value. My friends can't imagine a life without sex, and much less can they imagine a life without wanting any. To them the very notion seems absurd. It is their version of hell on earth (or close to it, by the sound of things), and yet I see their lives, their levels of stress, and their obsessions, and I can't imagine ever trading my inner peace for something like that. I can't imagine anything that would make it worth it.

I may be blind, I may be missing the beauty of the sunsets, but I don't miss the ability to see the different races, or rather the hatred that ability engenders.